LITTLE LORD FAUNTLEROY

Cedric Errol lives with his American mother in New York. His father came from England, but he died some years ago, and Cedric knows nothing about his father's family. But one day an English lawyer comes to New York. He is Mr Havisham, lawyer to the Earl of Dorincourt, and he has news for Cedric and his mother. The Earl is Cedric's grandfather, and because Cedric's father is dead, Cedric is now the heir to the Dorincourt riches and family name. He must leave New York, say goodbye to his friends Mr Hobbs the grocery-man and Dick the boot-black, and go to England. As the Earl's grandson, his name is now Lord Fauntleroy, and he must live in a castle with his rich old grandfather.

But rich people are not always happy people, or nice people. The Earl of Dorincourt is an angry, selfish, bad- tempered old man, and he hates America and Americans. Everyone is afraid of him. But to Cedric, a grandfather is someone to love, and the Earl has a lot to learn from his American grandson . . .

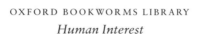

OXFORD BOOKWORMS LIBRARY
Human Interest

Little Lord Fauntleroy

Stage 1 (400 headwords)

Series Editor: Jennifer Bassett
Founder Editor: Tricia Hedge
Activities Editors: Jennifer Bassett and Christine Lindop

FRANCES HODGSON BURNETT

Little Lord Fauntleroy

Retold by
Jennifer Bassett

Illustrated by
Roberto Tomei

OXFORD UNIVERSITY PRESS

OXFORD
UNIVERSITY PRESS

Great Clarendon Street, Oxford OX2 6DP

Oxford University Press is a department of the University of Oxford.
It furthers the University's objective of excellence in research, scholarship,
and education by publishing worldwide in

Oxford New York

Auckland Cape Town Dar es Salaam Hong Kong Karachi
Kuala Lumpur Madrid Melbourne Mexico City Nairobi
New Delhi Shanghai Taipei Toronto

With offices in

Argentina Austria Brazil Chile Czech Republic France Greece
Guatemala Hungary Italy Japan Poland Portugal Singapore
South Korea Switzerland Thailand Turkey Ukraine Vietnam

OXFORD and OXFORD ENGLISH are registered trade marks of
Oxford University Press in the UK and in certain other countries

ISBN: 978 0 19 478929 5

A complete recording of this Bookworms edition of
Little Lord Fauntleroy is available

Printed in China

acknowledgements
Illustrations by: Roberto Tomei/Beehive

Word count (main text): 7, 250 words

For more information on the Oxford Bookworms Library,
visit www.oup.com/bookworms

CONTENTS

PEOPLE IN THIS STORY

Cedric (Ceddie) Errol, Lord Fauntleroy, *grandson of the Earl of Dorincourt*

Mrs Errol (Dearest), *Cedric's mother, and wife of the youngest son of the Earl of Dorincourt*

Mr Errol, *(now dead) Cedric's father, and the youngest son of the Earl*

IN AMERICA

Mr Hobbs, *a man with a grocery store in Cedric's street; a friend of Cedric's*

Dick, *a boot-black; a friend of Cedric's*

Ben, *Dick's brother, living in California*

Minna, *Ben's wife, address unknown*

Bridget, *a woman with twelve children; a friend of Cedric's*

IN ENGLAND

The Earl of Dorincourt, *Cedric's grandfather*

Bevis
Maurice } *(now dead) the two older sons of the Earl*

Mr Havisham, *lawyer for the Earl of Dorincourt*

Mr Newick, *rent collector for the Earl of Dorincourt*

Mr Dawson, *vicar at Dorincourt*

Mr Higgins, *a farmer at Dorincourt*

Servants at Dorincourt Castle

Villagers at Dorincourt

CHAPTER I

A big surprise

Cedric Errol and his mamma were very good friends.
This was important because there were only two of
them. Cedric's father was dead, and it was a sad day in
the little house in New York when Mrs Errol told Cedric
this news.

'Dear, dear Ceddie,' she said. 'Your papa was very ill
last week and – and he – he's not coming home to us.
He's never coming home again because . . .' And then
she began to cry.

Cedric was only seven years old, but he was a very
loving little boy. He went at once to his mamma and put
his little arms around her and his face next to her face.
They did not need any more words.

So Cedric and his mother were alone in the world. Mrs
Errol's mother and father were dead, and Mr Errol's
family was in England. Mr Errol's father – Cedric's
grandfather – was an important man. He was the Earl
of Dorincourt, the head of one of the oldest and most
famous families in England. He lived at Dorincourt
Castle, and was very rich.

But he was not a nice person. He was an angry, bad-

The Earl of Dorincourt was an angry, bad-tempered old man.

tempered old man – and he hated America and Americans. So when his youngest son, Cedric's father, married an American girl in New York, a girl without money or family, just a nobody, the Earl was very angry. He wrote this letter to his son:

Never come to Dorincourt Castle, and never write to
me. I don't want to see you again. Don't ask me for
help or money. You can live – or die; I don't want to
know. You are no longer my son.

The Earl had two older sons, but they were bad, selfish
men. They spent the Earl's money on horses and women,
never said a kind word, or did a good thing in their lives.
Nobody liked them, and their father hated them. They
were a black page in the book of the Dorincourt family.

Cedric's father was very different from his brothers.
He had a beautiful face, was tall and strong, and had the
kindest heart in the world. Everybody loved him.

He was very sad when his father's angry letter arrived.
He loved his home in England, and he even loved his
bad-tempered old father. But he was young and happy
with his sweet young wife.

Soon Cedric arrived, and there never was a happier
child than little Ceddie. He slept well, he ate well, he
smiled a lot, and never cried. And he had big brown eyes
and beautiful golden-yellow hair.

When he was older, he still smiled a lot, and he was
the happiest, friendliest little boy in the world. Everybody
liked him. Everybody liked to talk to him when they met
him in the street. He had some good friends. There was
Mr Hobbs, the grocery-man in the store at the end of
their street. There were the children along the street, and
there was Dick, the boot-black boy. And there was

Bridget. Bridget had twelve children, and her husband was a builder. But he was often ill and could not work, and then there was no money for the rent. Cedric felt very sorry for them all when life was difficult.

Cedric's best friend was his mamma. Her eyes were sad, and she always wore a black dress, but she was young and pretty, and she loved her little boy very much.

So life went on for Cedric Errol and his friends. Then one day everything changed. Mrs Errol had a visitor from England. He was a tall old man, in dark clothes. His name was Mr Havisham, and he was the lawyer for the Earl of Dorincourt. He had some very surprising news for Cedric's mother.

'You know that the Earl had three sons, Mrs Errol,' he said. 'The two older sons, Bevis and Maurice, died two or three months ago – one in an accident, and the other from an illness. They were not married and they had no children. Your husband is dead too, and so his son is now the heir. Cedric Errol is now Lord Fauntleroy and the next Earl of Dorincourt after his grandfather dies.'

Mrs Errol's face went very white. 'Oh,' she said, 'is the Earl going to take Cedric away from me? We are so happy together. I try to be a good mother to him.'

Mr Havisham was not a family man. He was a lawyer, a cold man of business, but he saw that Mrs Errol was a loving mother. His next news was difficult to say.

'I must tell you, Mrs Errol,' he said, 'that the Earl is

not very friendly to you. He does not like America or Americans, and he was very angry when his son married you. I am sorry to say this, but he does not want to see you. He wants Lord Fauntleroy to live with him at Dorincourt Castle, but he wants you to live in a different

Cedric's best friend was his mamma.

house. He is giving you a house called Court Lodge, and there Lord Fauntleroy can visit you every day.'

Mr Havisham watched Mrs Errol carefully. 'Is she going to cry?' he thought. He did not know the right words to say to a crying woman.

But Mrs Errol did not cry. She stood for a moment at the window, then turned and looked at the lawyer.

'My husband loved Dorincourt,' she said quietly. 'He loved England, and everything English. He was very sad to leave it all. So I think Ceddie must go back, and learn how to be an English earl.'

She looked at the lawyer with her sweet, sad eyes. 'I hope the Earl can learn to love Ceddie. He is only little, and he is a very loving child.'

Mr Havisham thought about the old Earl. He was a bad-tempered, selfish old man, and did not love anyone. But the lawyer did not say this.

'Mrs Errol,' he said, 'the Earl wants the best of everything for his grandson. He wants him to be happy. Your son is going to have a very good life at Dorincourt.'

A short time later Cedric came home from a visit to his friend Mr Hobbs, the grocery-man. He was very surprised to find a visitor in the sitting room. His mother ran to him and took his hands.

'Oh Ceddie,' she cried. 'Dear, dear Ceddie!'

Mr Havisham stood up and looked down at Cedric. 'And so this,' he said slowly, 'is little Lord Fauntleroy.'

CHAPTER 2

Saying goodbye to America

*I*t was a lot of news for a seven-year-old boy – uncles dying, an English grandfather, a new home in England, a new name . . . He did not understand it all at first. And when he did, he was not very happy.

'Oh, Dearest,' he said to his mother. (Cedric's father always called her 'Dearest', and so the little boy used the name too.) 'I don't think I want to be an earl. None of the boys in our street are earls. Please can I *not* be one?'

'Your papa loved his home in England, Ceddie,' said his mother. 'I think he would like you to go there, and be an earl one day.'

'I'm sorry to leave all my friends. Dick, and Bridget, and everyone,' said Cedric sadly. 'And Mr Hobbs isn't going to like the news. He says kings and lords are all bad people. America has a president, and Mr Hobbs says presidents are much better than kings.'

The next day Cedric went to see Mr Hobbs at his grocery store. He sat down in his usual place, but at first he could not find the words to tell Mr Hobbs his news. Then he said it all at once, very quickly.

Mr Hobbs stared at him. 'Well!' he said. 'Can this be true?'

'Yes, Mr Hobbs,' said Cedric. 'I'm sorry to say it's all true. Mr Havisham says I am Lord Fauntleroy now, and one day I'm going to be the Earl of Dorincourt, after my grandfather dies.'

'Well!' said Mr Hobbs. 'Well, well, well!'

They talked about it for a long time, and in the end Mr Hobbs was happier about lords and earls. He liked his young friend very much. He first knew Cedric when he was six weeks old, and he had a grandfatherly interest in the boy. But he did not like Cedric going to England.

'Well!' said Mr Hobbs. 'Well, well, well!'

'Can't you stay here and be an earl?' he asked.

'No, I can't,' said Cedric sadly. 'Dearest says we must go to England.'

The Dorincourt name was an old and famous one, and the family was very rich, with great houses and castles in England. Mr Havisham, the family's lawyer for forty years, knew the Earl very well. He remembered the Earl's words to him before he left England.

I hate that American woman. She married my son because he was an earl's son, and she wanted to be rich. Her son is going to be just like her.

But after a week in New York Mr Havisham knew differently. 'Mrs Errol married the Earl's son because she loved him with all her heart,' he thought. 'She's not interested in money, she asks nothing for herself. She only wants her little boy to be happy. I think the Earl is wrong about her, and about her little boy.'

Mr Havisham was surprised and pleased by the new Lord Fauntleroy. Cedric was a fine boy, tall and strong, with his mother's brown eyes and his father's golden hair. He spoke well, was not afraid of anything, and was friendly with everyone. He had a kind heart, too. Mr Havisham learnt that very soon.

One day he was with Cedric when his mother was out. Mr Havisham wanted to talk to him about his new life in England. But Cedric spoke first.

'Please, what is an earl?' he asked. 'I don't know anything about them. Please can you tell me?'

'An earl is – is a very important person,' Mr Havisham said. 'He usually comes from a very old family. The first Earl of Dorincourt lived four hundred years ago.'

'Well, well!' said Cedric. 'That was a long time ago. That's interesting. But what does an earl do?'

This was not an easy question to answer. 'An earl,' Mr Havisham began, 'um . . . an earl often helps the king. Perhaps he's a soldier for the king. Some earls were very brave men in the old days.'

'Oh,' said Cedric. 'My papa was a soldier, and he was a very brave man, you know. I'm pleased earls are brave. It's a good thing to be brave, don't you think?'

'Yes,' Mr Havisham said. 'There is another good thing about earls. Some of them have money – a lot of money.'

'That's a good thing to have,' said Cedric. 'I'd like a lot of money.'

'Would you?' said Mr Havisham. 'Why?'

'Well,' Cedric said, happily, 'a person can do so many things with money, you see. I can buy beautiful things for Dearest, like books and pretty dresses. I can buy a warm winter coat for Bridget – she lives in our street and has twelve children. And a present for Mr Hobbs at the grocery store. And then for Dick—'

'Who is Dick?' asked Mr Havisham.

'Dick is a boot-black,' said Lord Fauntleroy. 'He cleans

people's boots in the street, you know. He's one of the nicest people in the world. When I was little, he was very kind to me once. And when someone is kind to you, you never forget it, do you?'

'And what would you like to do for Dick?' asked the lawyer. He smiled a little smile. A boot-black, a grocery-man, a poor woman with twelve children – strange friends for the grandson of an earl.

'Buy the business for him,' said the young lord happily. 'He works for Jake now, and Jake is no good, you see. Dick does all the work and Jake takes all the money. Dick gets so angry! Dick needs new brushes, and new clothes, and a sign, and then he can get somewhere!'

'Dick is a boot-black. He cleans people's boots in the street.'

At that moment Mrs Errol came home. 'I am so sorry to be late,' she said. 'I was at the house of a friend. Her husband is ill, and she needs help, poor thing.'

'Oh,' cried the young lord. He jumped up from his chair. 'That's Bridget. I must visit her too.'

'One moment,' said the lawyer. He remembered the Earl's words. *The boy can have anything. Tell him that. Put money in his pockets, and tell him it came from his grandfather.* Mr Havisham told Mrs Errol and Cedric about the Earl's money, but he said it more kindly.

Then he asked, 'So, would Lord Fauntleroy like to help this poor woman?'

At first Cedric did not understand.

His mother put her arms around him. 'Ceddie dear,' she said, 'the Earl is your grandpapa, your papa's father. He's very kind, and he loves you and he wants you to love him. He wants you to be happy and to make other people happy. He's very rich, and he gave Mr Havisham some money for you. You can give some to Bridget now, to pay her rent and to buy food for her husband and her children. Isn't that fine, Ceddie? Isn't he good?'

Cedric's face was suddenly very excited. He looked from his mother to Mr Havisham.

'Can I have it now?' he cried. 'Can I run to her house and give it to her this minute?'

Mr Havisham gave Cedric twenty-five dollars, and Cedric was out of the house in seconds.

'You can give some money to Bridget now,' said his mother.

A short time later Cedric was back, with a big smile on his face. 'Bridget cried,' he said. 'She cried because she was so happy. I think I'm going to like being an earl.'

The old lawyer smiled his little smile again. 'What's the Earl going to think about that?' he thought. 'He gives his grandson money, and the boy gives it to a poor woman to pay her rent.'

The day for leaving New York came quickly. In the last days Lord Fauntleroy was very busy. With the Earl's money, Bridget's children all had new clothes, and Mr Hobbs had a very fine gold watch from his little friend.

'Look,' said Cedric. 'The watch has our names on the back. So you can't forget me!'

Mr Hobbs held the watch in his hand, and at first he could not speak. 'I'm not going to forget you, my boy,' he said at last. 'You never forget a good friend, do you?'

Dick, too, could not find words at first to thank his little friend. He now had new brushes, a big new sign, and the best boot-black business in New York. On the last day he came to the house to say goodbye.

'I'm sorry he's going away, I really am,' he said to Mr Havisham. 'I never had a friend like him.' Dick shook Cedric's hand for a long time. 'Goodbye,' he said. 'Write and tell me all about it, earls and everything.'

That evening Cedric's mamma was very quiet.

Cedric held her hand. 'It's sad saying goodbye to all our friends and our little house, isn't it, Dearest?' he said.

'Yes, Ceddie dear, it is,' she said. 'Very, very sad.'

CHAPTER 3

A new life in England

The ship from New York to England took eleven days, and the young Lord Fauntleroy made a lot of friends in that time. Everybody liked him, and everybody was interested in the story of his family.

Cedric learnt a new piece of the story on the ship.

'We're going to have different homes, Ceddie,' his mother told him. 'You must live in the castle with your grandfather, and I have a little house called Court Lodge not far away. You can run in and see me every day.'

'We're going to have different homes, Ceddie,' his mother said.

Cedric could not understand this, and was very unhappy about it. 'But why?' he asked again and again.

'When you are older,' his mother said sadly, 'I can tell you. But not now.'

To Mr Havisham she said this. 'The Earl hates me, and does not want to see me. I don't want Cedric to know that, because how could he understand it? He is a loving child, and I want him and his grandfather to be friends. It is better for the Earl that way.'

'I don't like it,' Cedric said later to Mr Havisham. 'But Dearest tells me I must live with my grandfather, because, you see, all his children are dead. You must be sorry for a man when all his children are dead.'

Mr Havisham smiled. He enjoyed his little talks with Cedric very much.

'Are you going to like the Earl?' he asked.

'Yes,' said Lord Fauntleroy. 'Of course a boy must like his grandfather. And he's very kind to me.'

On his first night in England Cedric stayed with his mother in her little house near the castle. But Mr Havisham went up to the castle to see the Earl.

The Earl was in a big chair by the fire. He had a bad right foot, and it gave him a lot of pain. And when his foot was painful, the Earl was even more bad-tempered than usual.

'Well, Havisham,' he said. 'What's the news?'

Mr Havisham began to tell him about the ship, but the Earl did not want to hear about that.

'Yes, yes, yes,' he said angrily. 'But what about the boy? What kind of a boy is he? Is he stupid? What does he look like? Does he talk all the time, in that stupid noisy American way?'

Mr Havisham smiled his little lawyer's smile. 'He is different from most English children, I think. But one thing, my lord. The boy knows nothing about your feelings about his mother. She said nothing to him, because she wants you and him to be friends. So, he thinks you are the kindest grandfather in the world.'

'He does, eh?' said the Earl.

'What kind of a boy is he? Is he stupid?' said the Earl.

'So when you speak of his mother, please be careful.'

'Huh!' said the Earl. 'The boy's only seven years old.'

'Those seven years were all at his mother's side,' said Mr Havisham. 'And she has all his love.'

The next afternoon the Earl's carriage carried Lord Fauntleroy and Mr Havisham up to Dorincourt Castle. At the great front door all the servants of the house waited to see the new Lord Fauntleroy, the little boy from America. When Cedric got out of the carriage, everybody had something to say about him.

'Oh, look! He's just like his father, with the same hair, the same eyes. The dear little boy!'

'And he's got his father's happy smile too – look!'

'I'm sorry for him, living with that bad-tempered old man. Nobody ever gets a kind word out of the Earl!'

'And his poor young mother, living all alone at Court Lodge, without her little boy! I'm sorry for her, too.'

Cedric smiled and said hello to everybody, in his usual friendly way, and went into the house with Mr Havisham. One of the servants, a tall young man, took Cedric to the back of the house and opened a door.

'Lord Fauntleroy, my lord,' he said.

Cedric walked down a long room to a fire at the end. There was a big chair there, and an old man in it, with white hair and black eyes.

Cedric came close to the chair. 'Are you the Earl?' he

Cedric smiled and said hello to everybody, in his usual friendly way.

said. 'I'm your grandson. Mr Havisham brought me.' He held out his hand. 'I'm very happy to see you.'

The Earl shook hands with him, very surprised. He stared at the strong, beautiful little boy in front of him, with his golden curly hair and his friendly open face.

'Happy to see me, are you?' he said.

'Yes,' said Lord Fauntleroy. 'Of course. Everybody loves their family, don't they? It's exciting to meet a new grandfather. And you are very kind!'

He sat down on a chair and looked at his grandfather with great interest. The old Earl looked back at him. He did not like anybody in his family. He was bad-tempered with them all, and they all hated him.

'Kind?' he said. 'How am I kind?'

'Because of the money,' Cedric said happily. 'For Bridget, and Dick. I wanted to thank you.'

'Bridget? Dick? Who are they?' said the Earl.

And so Lord Fauntleroy told his grandfather all about his friends in New York, about Bridget and her husband and her twelve children, about Dick and Jake and the boot-black business.

The Earl of Dorincourt did not like children, and children were usually afraid of him. But Cedric was not afraid, and he talked in his usual friendly way.

'He thinks I'm his friend,' thought the Earl. 'And he wants to please me.' This was a new feeling for the Earl. Cedric was only a little boy from America, but perhaps it was nice for the Earl to see a smiling face for once.

They talked all evening, through dinner, and after dinner. In the end Cedric went to sleep in front of the fire. The Earl called a servant.

'Carry Lord Fauntleroy up to his bedroom,' he said. 'Be careful with him. The boy's tired.'

CHAPTER 4

The Earl and his grandson

*T*he next morning there were more surprises for Cedric. He had a servant, Mary, and three rooms in the castle – a room to sleep in, a room to have breakfast in, and a room full of books and toys and games. Wonderful games! Later, when he went down to the Earl in the long room, he took one of the games with him.

'Thank you very much for all the wonderful things. You're so kind!' Cedric said happily. 'This game is really good! Would you like to play it with me?'

'Would you like to play this game with me?' said Cedric.

The Earl was in a bad temper and his foot was painful. He did not give money and toys to his grandson because he had a kind heart. He gave these things because he wanted the boy to forget his mother. He opened his mouth to say, *No. I don't play children's games.* But he did not say it. He said, 'Very well. You can teach me.'

When the tall young servant came in with a visitor, Mr Dawson the vicar, they heard excited cries and laughing.

'That's two out! Bad luck, grandfather!'

Mr Dawson usually hated his visits to the old Earl, but today was different, and surprising.

'Good morning, Dawson,' the Earl said. 'My grandson is keeping me busy.' He put his hand on Cedric's head and nearly smiled. 'What is it today, Dawson?'

'It's Higgins of Edge Farm, my lord,' said Mr Dawson. 'He can't pay his rent. He needs more time.'

Every house in the village and every farm for miles around Dorincourt all belonged to the Earl. The villagers and the farmers paid their rent to the Earl's man, Mr Newick. And Mr Newick was a hard man. Mr Dawson came to the Earl many times a year, with the same question. 'Can this family or that family have more time to pay their rent?' And the answer was always 'no'.

'Higgins?' said the Earl. 'He's a bad farmer, and he's always late with his rent, Newick tells me.'

'His wife is ill, and two of his children,' Mr Dawson said. 'And Newick wants to put them all out of the house into the street. Higgins came to me yesterday, to ask for help. Another month, he says, and he can find the rent.'

'Huh. They all say that,' said the Earl, looking angry.

Lord Fauntleroy listened to every word of this. He began to feel a great interest in Higgins and his family.

'It was the same for Bridget and her family,' he said.

The Earl jumped a little. 'I forgot *you*!' he said. 'I forgot we had a philanthropist in the room.' He stared at the boy for a minute. 'Come here,' he said.

Cedric went and stood next to him.

'What shall we do about Higgins, then?' said the Earl. 'Tell me.'

'What shall we do about Higgins, then?' said the Earl.

Mr Dawson began to feel worried. How could a seven-year-old child answer a question like that?

Lord Fauntleroy put his hand on his grandfather's arm. 'Well, I'm just a little boy, so what can I do? But *you* can do anything,' he said. 'Who's Newick?'

'He works for me,' said the Earl. 'And some of my villagers don't like him very much.'

'Are you going to write to him now?' Cedric asked. 'Shall I bring you a pen and some paper?'

In Cedric's world, there was only one answer to the question about Higgins. Of course, he must have more time. Of course, Newick must leave the family alone.

The Earl looked at him. 'Can you write?' he asked.

'Yes,' said Cedric, 'but not very well.'

'Bring the pen and paper, and you write the letter.'

Lord Fauntleroy's face went red. 'But my spelling isn't very good,' he said.

The Earl smiled a little. 'Higgins isn't interested in your spelling. I'm not the philanthropist; you are.'

And so Cedric wrote a letter to Mr Newick. It was true, the spelling was not very good.

Dear mr Newik, pleas leve mr higins alone for now, he can pay wen he is redy. Yors, Fauntleroy

Mr Dawson went away and took the letter for Mr Newick with him. He took a happy heart with him too. There were changes at Dorincourt Castle.

After Mr Dawson's visit, Cedric looked at the clock.

'Can I go to Dearest now?' he said to his grandfather. 'She's waiting for me.'

'There is something for you to see first,' said the Earl.

'Thank you,' said Fauntleroy, his face red again. 'But I think I must see it tomorrow. Dearest is waiting.'

'Very well,' said the Earl. Then he said, 'It's a pony.'

'A pony!' cried Fauntleroy. 'Is it a pony for me? Like the things in my room upstairs?'

'Yes,' said his grandfather. 'Would you like to see it?'

'A pony!' Fauntleroy said again. He was very excited. 'How kind you are! You give me everything. I *want* to see it very much, but . . . but there isn't time now.'

'Perhaps you can go to see your mother another time,' said the Earl. 'Tomorrow, or the day after.'

'Oh no,' said the boy. 'She thinks about me all the time, and I think about her too. I must go now.'

They went down to Court Lodge in the Earl's carriage. Cedric talked all the time, very happily.

'You're a very kind man, grandfather. You're always doing good things, and thinking about other

'It's a pony.'

people.' He counted on his fingers. 'Do you know, twenty-seven people are happy because of you. Twenty-seven!'

The Earl said nothing. He thought about his life – a rich, selfish, bad-tempered life, without friends or loving family. *When did I say a kind word, or do a good thing? Now this child is calling me kind, and good, and I know that is not true.* These were new thoughts for the Earl, and he did not like them.

When they arrived at Court Lodge, Cedric was out of the carriage in a second, running to the front door. The Earl watched from the carriage. The door opened, and a young, pretty woman in black ran out. Cedric jumped into her arms, smiling and laughing. The Earl closed the window and his carriage drove away.

The Earl watched from the carriage.

CHAPTER 5

News from Mr Havisham

*T*he news went round the village and the farms faster than a carriage with six horses.

'Did you hear? The vicar went up to the castle and spoke to the Earl about poor Mr Higgins . . .'

'And the boy was there, little Lord Fauntleroy . . .'

'Yes, and the Earl said to his grandson, "You write to Mr Newick, you tell him." And the boy did!'

'And the vicar took the letter to Mr Newick, and now Mr Newick can't put poor Higgins and his family out in the street.'

'Yes, and they've got another month to find the rent!'

Days and weeks went past, and by now everybody knew about Lord Fauntleroy and his mother. They loved the boy, with his golden curly hair and his happy smile. They saw him every day on his new pony, and he always had a friendly word for everyone.

The village people loved Mrs Errol too, because of her kind heart and her sweet face. When somebody was ill in the village, Mrs Errol was always there to help.

But the Earl never saw her, never spoke to her, never went to her house. Cedric, of course, saw her every day, but his heart was sad because his 'best friend' did not live with him in the same house.

The Earl liked his little grandson more and more every week. He often forgot about his painful foot, and he began to smile more; sometimes he even laughed. He liked to please his grandson. When Lord Fauntleroy

Cedric was sad because his mother did not live with him.

wanted new houses for some very poor villagers, the Earl built new houses. When the boy wanted to talk about his mother, the Earl listened. But he did not like it.

'Do you *never* forget about your mother?' he said to his grandson one day.

'No,' said Cedric. 'Never. And she never forgets about me. I don't forget about *you*, you know, when I'm away.'

The young lord did not forget his friends in America either. Letters went to and from New York, and Dick and Mr Hobbs heard all about Cedric's new life.

One day the Earl gave a great party, and all the important families for miles around came to it – to meet Lord Fauntleroy. Mr Havisham came from London too, but he was very quiet all evening, and looked worried.

At the end of the party, the Earl spoke to him.

'Well, Havisham, what's the matter?'

'I bring some bad news, my lord, about your heir.'

'My heir? Fauntleroy is my heir. What do you mean?'

'My lord,' said Mr Havisham. 'Cedric Errol is not your heir. He is not Lord Fauntleroy. The true Lord Fauntleroy is the son of your oldest son Bevis, and at the moment he is in London with his mother.'

The Earl's face was as white as his hair. 'Bevis?' he said. 'This isn't true. Havisham, tell me this isn't true!'

'A woman came to my office this morning,' said Mr Havisham. 'Bevis married her six years ago in London. She has all the papers. He left her after a year, but she

The Earl began to walk up and down the room.

had a son. He's now five years old. The woman is
American. She's beautiful, but . . . well, she can only just
write her name. And she's only interested in the money.'

The Earl's face was now dark red. He jumped up from

his chair and began to walk up and down the room.

'Bevis was always the worst!' he said angrily. 'I hated him, and he hated me. I must stop this! Cedric is very dear to me, Havisham, very dear. He's a fine boy, and he's going to be a better Earl of Dorincourt than me – or any child of Bevis's!'

Far away in New York, two of Cedric's friends sat round a table in a grocery store. They ate a supper of bread and cold meat, and talked about Lord Fauntleroy.

Dick usually came round to the grocery store once a week. He and Mr Hobbs were now good friends, and they enjoyed reading the letters from England, and talking about them. When they wrote back to Cedric, Mr Hobbs helped Dick with his writing, because writing was difficult for Dick.

'I didn't get much time for school, see,' Dick told Mr Hobbs one day. 'Pa and Ma were dead, and there was no money. So me and my brother worked.'

'That was your brother Ben, was it?' Mr Hobbs said.

'Yeah, my older brother,' said Dick. 'He was good to me, Ben was. But then he married this girl, and oh dear, she was bad news! She was a good-looking girl – big black eyes, long black hair – but she was always angry about something or somebody, me or Ben or the baby. I remember, she broke a plate on Ben's head once. She hit the baby too. A nice mother she was!'

'Women!' said Mr Hobbs. 'Best to keep away from them, I say. I never married.'

'Well, she didn't stay long,' Dick said. 'She was angry with Ben because he didn't make money faster. So one day she left, with the baby. We never saw her again. She left New York, someone told us.'

'What happened to your brother?' Mr Hobbs asked.

'Ben's out in California now, working with horses on a big farm somewhere. He was sad about Minna and his baby son for a long time, poor old Ben.'

After supper, Mr Hobbs took out a letter. 'This came from our friend today,' he said. 'Let's read it together now.' He opened the letter and they began to read.

My dear frend Mr Hobbs – i have some surprising news to tel you and Dick. I am not lord fauntleroy becaus my uncle Bevis (he is dead) had a litle boy but nobody knew about him. my uncle Bevis was the oldest son of the earl and so his son is lord fauntleroy and i am just Cedric Errol again. my papa was the youngest son and youngest sons don't have anything so i am not very rich and i am going to learn to work prhaps with horses because i like them a lot. my grandfarther is very angry about it and i never saw him angry before. with love from yor old frend Cedric Errol (not lord fauntleroy).

'Well!' said Mr Hobbs. 'Well, I don't know. Did you ever hear anything like that before?'

'No, I didn't,' said Dick. 'But I know one thing. Young Cedric needs his friends at a time like this. Let's write back to him, Mr Hobbs, and let's do it now!'

Mr Hobbs opened the letter and they began to read.

CHAPTER 6

News from America

*T*he story about the new Lord Fauntleroy was soon in all the newspapers in England. And in Dorincourt village, of course, nobody could stop talking about it.

'The Earl is so angry about it! He doesn't like the woman, and he doesn't want the boy!'

'Yes, and they say he's got twenty lawyers in London, all working on it, looking into things, asking questions.'

'Did you see the woman, Bevis's wife, when she came to the castle with her boy? She's a tall, black-eyed thing, with a hard face. Not a nice woman, and nothing like our sweet, kind Mrs Errol. And the boy's nothing, when you think about our dear little lord.'

'How's it all going to end?'

'Who knows?'

When the Earl told Lord Fauntleroy the news, the boy listened carefully. Then he asked, with a worried look in his big brown eyes:

'Can they take Dearest's house away from her?'

'*No!*' the Earl said. 'They can take nothing from her.'

'Ah,' said Cedric. 'I'm so pleased about that.' He thought for a minute, then looked up at his grandfather.

In Dorincourt village nobody could stop talking about it.

'And . . . that other boy,' he said, a little shakily, 'he's going to be your boy now, and live with you, isn't he?'

'NO!' the Earl said again. 'No, he's not!'

Cedric was very surprised. He jumped up from his chair and began to smile. 'Can I still be your boy, then? I'm not going to be an earl one day, but that doesn't matter, does it? I just want to be your boy, always.'

The Earl looked down at his little grandson. 'My boy!' he said, and – this is true – *his* voice was a little shaky too. And there was something in those old angry black eyes, something new, something different. 'Yes, you're my boy, my only boy, the best boy in my life.'

Cedric's face went red, and he looked very happy. 'That's all right, then. I was a little worried, but not now.'

'It's more important for my son to be a true, kind, brave man, like his father,' said Mrs Errol.

The Earl put his hand on the boy's head. 'You are right for Dorincourt, and . . . well, who knows? But always remember, you are my boy, first and last.'

The Earl talked many times with Mr Havisham about Bevis's wife and son, and Mr Havisham talked with other lawyers in London. There were questions about the woman's story. When was her son born? Where was he born? She was Bevis's wife, because she had the marriage papers, but was all her story true?

Some days later a visitor came to Court Lodge. The servant, her eyes big with surprise, ran to find Mrs Errol.

'It's the Earl, Mrs Errol!' she said. 'The Earl's here!'

When Mrs Errol came into her sitting room, she found a tall old man with white hair. He stared at her.

'The boy is very like you,' he said.

'People say that, my lord,' Mrs Errol said.

'You don't want your son to be the Earl of Dorincourt, do you?' the Earl said.

'It's a fine thing to be an earl,' said Mrs Errol quietly. 'But it's more important for my son to be a true, kind, brave man, like his father.'

'Not like his grandfather, you mean,' said the Earl.

'I don't know his grandfather.' Mrs Errol looked up into his face. 'But I know that Cedric loves you.'

The Earl began to walk up and down the room. 'Yes, and the boy is very dear to me,' he said. 'I'm an old man, tired of life, but then I found someone to live for. And

now this other boy . . . Havisham told you about him.'
He came back and stood in front of Mrs Errol.

'I am miserable,' he said. 'Miserable!' خوف

Again, his voice was a little shaky. 'I hated you once. I
don't know why. I came to see you because you are like
the boy, and the boy loves you, and I love him. Be kind to
me, because of the boy.'

Mrs Errol had a kind, loving heart. She put her hand
on the Earl's arm. 'Why don't you sit down for a moment?
You are tired, and unhappy.'

The Earl sat down, and they drank tea together, and
talked. He watched her sweet face and listened to her
quiet voice, and he began to feel a little better. Before he
went away, he looked around the room.

'This is a happy room,' he said. 'Can I come again and
talk to you?'

'Of course, my lord. Come when you like.'

The English newspapers could not stop writing about
the Lord Fauntleroy story. And soon American
newspapers began to write about it too. Mr Hobbs read
everything, and he and Dick talked about it every day.

Dick was a very good boot-black, and a lot of people
came to him. One of them was a young lawyer, and one
day he gave Dick his newspaper. 'Here's a paper for you,
Dick,' he said. 'This one's got pictures in it – an English
castle, and this English Earl, and his son's wife. Well, she

says she's his son's wife, but the Earl says not. I don't –
hey, Dick, what's the matter?'

Dick stared at the picture in the newspaper with his
mouth open. He saw a good-looking young woman,
with black eyes and a lot of long black hair.

Dick stared at the picture in the newspaper with his mouth open.

The boy gives him hope for the future

'I know her!' he cried. 'I know her like the back of my hand. It's Minna! It's my brother Ben's wife.' He began to put away his brushes.

'Where are you going, Dick?' said the young lawyer.

'I'm off to my friend Mr Hobbs,' cried Dick. 'We've got business to do.'

And away he ran through the streets of New York to Mr Hobbs's grocery store. At first, Mr Hobbs could not understand it. 'But why did Minna do it?' he asked.

'Money!' said Dick. 'She always wanted money. She married this Bevis, the Earl's son, for money. And now she wants to get our Cedric's money. Well, she's not going to! You and me, Mr Hobbs, are going to stop her!'

Then Mr Hobbs and Dick began to think carefully.

'Dick, you write to Ben, and I'm going to write to Cedric,' said Mr Hobbs. 'And that Mr Havisham too.'

'Right,' said Dick. 'But we need help here, Mr Hobbs. This is lawyers' work. Why don't I ask that young lawyer, him with the newspaper?'

Dick's friend the young lawyer was very surprised by the story, but very interested. He began to get busy too, and letters went to California, to London, and to Dorincourt.

CHAPTER 7

Changes at the castle

Wonderful things always happen quickly. Letters went to and from America and England, and soon Mr Hobbs, Dick, and Dick's brother Ben were on a ship to England.

Things happened quickly because Minna – and it *was* Minna – was a bad woman, and a stupid one too. When she married Bevis, the Earl's son, she was still Ben's wife, and you can't have two husbands. Her son Tom was eight years old, not five, so he was Ben's son, not Bevis's son.

She was in a sitting room in the Dorincourt Hotel when the end came. The door opened, and in came three people – Mr Havisham, a big young man, and the Earl of Dorincourt. Minna jumped to her feet with a cry.

'Do you know this woman?' Mr Havisham said to the big young man.

'Yes,' said Ben. 'I know her and she knows me.'

And that was the end of Minna. She left the hotel and nobody ever saw her again. Ben took his son Tom back to California with him, and with the Earl's help he bought a little farm there.

When the Earl left the hotel, he went at once to his carriage. 'To Court Lodge,' he said to his servant.

He came into the sitting room at Court Lodge and found Cedric with his mother. The Earl looked taller and younger, and there was a smile in his black eyes. He looked at his grandson.

'So here,' he said, 'is Lord Fauntleroy.'

Mrs Errol stood up. 'Oh, is he truly Lord Fauntleroy?' she asked. The Earl took her hand.

'To live with us,' Cedric cried. 'To live with us always!'

'Yes,' he answered, 'he is.' Then he put his other hand on Cedric's head.

'Fauntleroy,' he said, 'ask your mother this. When is she coming to us at the castle?'

Lord Fauntleroy put his arms round his mother. 'To live with us,' he cried. 'To live with us always!'

Mrs Errol looked at the Earl with her sweet, sad eyes.

'We need you,' the Earl said. 'We need you very much.'

Dick and Mr Hobbs did not go back to America at once. The Earl had a talk with Dick, and Dick went back to school, in England this time. His writing got much better, and he began to study to be a lawyer.

Mr Hobbs liked England very much. In the end he opened a new shop in Dorincourt, and was an important person in the village. People at the castle, of course, always went to his shop, and Cedric was in and out every day, to see his old friend.

'Are you ever going back to America?' Dick asked Mr Hobbs when he visited one day.

'I don't think so,' Mr Hobbs said. 'I like to be near the boy, you see. He's a fine little lord, young Cedric.'

44

GLOSSARY

alone   without any other person

bad-tempered   often angry and impatient

belong   if something is yours, it belongs to you

boot-black   somebody who cleans people's shoes in the street

brave   ready to do dangerous or difficult things and not be afraid

busy   with a lot of things to do

curly   (of hair) with lots of little round shapes

dear / dearest   words for someone that you love

earl   a British title for a man from an old, important family

farm   land and buildings where people keep animals and grow food

feelings   something that you feel inside yourself, like happiness or sadness

fine *(adj)*   good, nice, beautiful, etc.

game *(illus)*   something you play that has rules

great   very big

grocery-man   a man who has a grocery store (a food shop)

hate *(v)*   to have a very strong feeling of not liking somebody

heart   the place inside you where your feelings are

heir   somebody who gets money, buildings, land, etc. when another person, usually in the same family, dies

jump *(v)*   to move very quickly and suddenly

kind   friendly and good to other people

lawyer   a person who knows about the law

lord   a British title for a man (or boy) from an important family; **my lord** words you use when you speak to lords, earls, etc.

marry   to take somebody as your husband or wife

miserable   feeling very unhappy

pain   a feeling in your body when you are hurt or ill

painful giving pain

philanthropist a rich person who helps the poor and those in need, often by giving money

poor (1) with very little money; (2) a word that you use when you feel sad for someone

pretty nice to look at

rent *(n)* money you pay to live in another person's house

sad not happy

selfish thinking too much about what you want, and not about what other people want

servant a person who works in another person's house

shake (past tense **shook**) to move quickly from side to side, or up and down

shaky *(adj)* shaking because you have strong feelings or are afraid

soldier a person in an army, who fights for their country

stare *(v)* to look at somebody or something for a long time

store *(n)* a shop

stupid not intelligent, not clever

surprise the feeling you have when something happens that you did not expect

surprised feeling or showing surprise

surprising making you feel surprise

sweet (of a person) pretty, kind

toy a thing for a child to play with

unhappy not happy

unkind not kind

vicar a priest in some Christian churches

worried unhappy because you think that something bad is going to happen

ACTIVITIES

Before Reading

1 **Read the back cover and the story introduction on the first page of the book. How much do you know now about the story? Tick one box for each sentence.**

YES NO

1 Cedric and his mother are very rich. ☐ ☒

2 Cedric's father is dead. ☒ ☐

3 Everybody likes the Earl of Dorincourt. ☐ ☒

4 Cedric's father was the Earl's son. ☒ ☐

5 Cedric must go to live in England. ☒ ☐

6 Dick and Mr Hobbs go with Cedric to England. ☐ ☒

7 Cedric's new name is Lord Fauntleroy. ☒ ☐

2 **What is going to happen in this story? Can you guess? Tick one box for each sentence.**

YES NO

1 The Earl is very unkind to Cedric. ☒ ☐

2 Cedric and his grandfather are soon good friends. ☒ ☐

3 Cedric's mother lives alone in a different house. ☐ ☒

4 The Earl loses all his money. ☒ ☐

5 Cedric dies and everybody is unhappy. ☐ ☒

6 Cedric and his mother go back to America. ☒ ☐

7 The story has a happy ending. ☒ ☐

ACTIVITIES

While Reading

Read chapters 1 to 3, and then complete these sentences with the right words.

afraid, bad-tempered, dead, friendly, sad, selfish, surprising

1 Mr Havisham brought some *surprising* news to New York.
2 Everybody liked Cedric because he was a *friendly* boy.
3 Mrs Errol was *sad* because her husband was *dead*.
4 The Earl was a *bad*, *tempered* man and nobody liked him.
5 Cedric liked his grandfather and was not *afraid* of him.

Read Chapters 4 to 6. Who said this, and to whom?

1 'What shall we do about Higgins, then? Tell me.'
2 'You're always doing good things.'
3 'I bring some bad news . . . about your heir.'
4 'I hated you once. I don't know why.'
5 'Money! She always wanted money.'

Before you read Chapter 7, think about the ending. What's going to happen? Can you guess? Choose some answers.

1 The real Lord Fauntleroy is . . .
   a) Minna's son.   b) Cedric.
2 Mrs Errol leaves her house and goes to live with . . .
   a) the Earl and Cedric.   b) a new husband.

ACTIVITIES

After Reading

1 Match the people with the sentences. Then use the sentences to write a description of each person. Use pronouns (*he, she*) and linking words (*and, but, because, so*) where possible.

Mrs Errol / Cedric / the Earl / Mr Hobbs / Dick

Example: <u>Cedric</u> is a kind, friendly boy. <u>He</u> always wants to help his friends, <u>so he</u> . . .

1 *Mr Hobbs* has a grocery store in New York.

2 *Cedric* is a kind, friendly boy.

3 *Dick* works as a boot-black in New York.

4 *Mrs Errol* does not want to live alone without her son.

5 *the Earl* gives money to his grandson.

6 *Cedric* sees a woman's picture in an American newspaper.

7 *Earl* wants Cedric to forget about his mother.

8 *Mrs Errol* wants Cedric to love his grandfather.

9 *Mr Hobbs* is very sorry when Cedric goes away to England.

10 *Cedric* always wants to help his friends.

11 *Mrs Errol* does not tell him about the Earl's feelings of hate for her.

12 *Cedric* is a much nicer person at the end of the story.

13 *Errol* gives the Earl's money to Bridget and her family.

14 *Hobbs* knows that the woman is his brother Ben's wife.

15 *Dick* likes Cedric's visits to his store.

2 Here is a new illustration for the story. Find the best place in the story to put the picture, and answer these questions.

The picture goes on page _3 5_.
1 Who are these three people? *cedric-mrHobbs-Dick*
2 Where are they going? *There going to England*
3 Why are they going there? *Beacuse Theyare working in the England whit Earl*

Now write a caption for the illustration.

Caption: _____

3 Look at Cedric's letter on page 32. His spelling is not very good. How many words are not spelt correctly? Count them, and then write the correct spellings.

1 There are __5__ words spelt incorrectly.
2 The correct spellings are: _surprising going to before to work about learn_

4 At the end of Chapter 6 Mr Hobbs and Dick wrote letters to Cedric and Ben. Use these words to complete their letters (one word for each gap).

ago, called, first, friend, hands, help, knows, letter, married, marry, news, two, who, woman, write, writing

1 Dear Cedric – we have important woman Who did your uncle Bevis first? The picture in our newspaper here is of a news called Minna. Dick letter her well, because she's the wife of his brother Ben and the mother of Ben's son. Minna left Ben many years ago. So married is the father of this new Lord Fauntleroy? Bevis or Ben? Dick is writing to Ben now. Wait for our next marry!

   Your good friend, Mr Hobbs

2 Dear Ben – Minna is in England. She called an Earl's son and had a son by him – she says. But she married you knows, and she can't have two husbands, can she? I think she wants to get her fat hands on the Earl of Dorincourt's money. The Earl is the grandfather of a boy _____ Cedric, you see, and young Cedric is a good

friend of me and Mr Hobbs. He went to England and
... Oh, it's a long story, Ben, I can't _write_ it all down.
Come to New York, quick! We need your _help_!

Your brother, Dick

5 Here is a puzzle. Look again at Activity 4, find the eight
'family' words in the letters, and fit them into this grid (all
words go across). Now find the hidden word in the grid.
Why is this word important in the story?

		A						
		O						
					O			
		U						

6 **What did you think about the people in this story? Choose
some names, and finish these sentences in your own words.**

*Cedric / Mrs Errol / the Earl of Dorincourt / Mr Havisham /
Mr Hobbs / Dick / Ben / Minna*

1 I felt sorry for _Mr Hobbs_ because _I go to England_.
2 I liked _cedric_ because _he is so friendly boy_
3 I didn't like _Earl_ because _he has bad tempered_
4 _Mr Havish_ was right to _the Earl_.
5 _minna_ was wrong to _the Havisham_

ABOUT THE AUTHOR

Frances Eliza Hodgson Burnett (1849–1924) was born in Manchester, England. When she was sixteen, her family went to the USA, and made their home in Knoxville, Tennessee. There, she began to write stories for magazines, because her family was poor and needed the money. She married in 1873, but went on writing, and her first novel, *That Lass o' Lowrie's*, came out in 1877. After that came more stories for adults and children, but in 1886 she wrote *Little Lord Fauntleroy*, and this book made her famous. The character of Cedric was based on her younger son, Vivian, and she read the story to him while she was writing it. Both Burnett boys called their mother 'Dearest'. Mrs Burnett's next famous book was *Sara Crewe* (1888), and this came out as a longer story called *A Little Princess* in 1905. There have been three films of this story.

Little Lord Fauntleroy and *A Little Princess* are about very nice, good children. Many parents at the time bought these books because they wanted their children to learn from the little lord and the 'little princess' how to be good. Mothers in America even dressed their sons in clothes like Lord Fauntleroy's.

Today, most people think that *The Secret Garden* (1910) is Mrs Burnett's best book. In this story the children are more like real children – they are difficult, they get angry, they shout and they scream. There are many films of this famous and much-loved story.

Frances Hodgson Burnett was a very popular writer in her time. She often came back to visit England, but she died in the USA, in a beautiful house on Long Island.

OXFORD BOOKWORMS LIBRARY

Classics • Crime & Mystery • Factfiles • Fantasy & Horror
Human Interest • Playscripts • Thriller & Adventure
True Stories • World Stories

The OXFORD BOOKWORMS LIBRARY provides enjoyable reading in English, with a wide range of classic and modern fiction, non-fiction, and plays. It includes original and adapted texts in seven carefully graded language stages, which take learners from beginner to advanced level. An overview is given on the next pages.

All Stage 1 titles are available as audio recordings, as well as over eighty other titles from Starter to Stage 6. All Starters and many titles at Stages 1 to 4 are specially recommended for younger learners. Every Bookworm is illustrated, and Starters and Factfiles have full-colour illustrations.

The OXFORD BOOKWORMS LIBRARY also offers extensive support. Each book contains an introduction to the story, notes about the author, a glossary, and activities. Additional resources include tests and worksheets, and answers for these and for the activities in the books. There is advice on running a class library, using audio recordings, and the many ways of using Oxford Bookworms in reading programmes. Resource materials are available on the website <www.oup.com/bookworms>.

The *Oxford Bookworms Collection* is a series for advanced learners. It consists of volumes of short stories by well-known authors, both classic and modern. Texts are not abridged or adapted in any way, but carefully selected to be accessible to the advanced student.

You can find details and a full list of titles in the *Oxford Bookworms Library Catalogue* and *Oxford English Language Teaching Catalogues*, and on the website <www.oup.com/bookworms>.

THE OXFORD BOOKWORMS LIBRARY
GRADING AND SAMPLE EXTRACTS

STARTER • 250 HEADWORDS
present simple – present continuous – imperative –
can/cannot, must – *going to* (future) – simple gerunds …

Her phone is ringing – but where is it?

Sally gets out of bed and looks in her bag. No phone. She looks under the bed. No phone. Then she looks behind the door. There is her phone. Sally picks up her phone and answers it. *Sally's Phone*

STAGE 1 • 400 HEADWORDS
… past simple – coordination with *and, but, or* –
subordination with *before, after, when, because, so* …

I knew him in Persia. He was a famous builder and I worked with him there. For a time I was his friend, but not for long. When he came to Paris, I came after him – I wanted to watch him. He was a very clever, very dangerous man. *The Phantom of the Opera*

STAGE 2 • 700 HEADWORDS
… present perfect – *will* (future) – *(don't) have to, must not, could* –
comparison of adjectives – simple *if* clauses – past continuous –
tag questions – *ask/tell* + infinitive …

While I was writing these words in my diary, I decided what to do. I must try to escape. I shall try to get down the wall outside. The window is high above the ground, but I have to try. I shall take some of the gold with me – if I escape, perhaps it will be helpful later. *Dracula*

STAGE 3 • 1000 HEADWORDS

… should, may – present perfect continuous – *used to* – past perfect –
causative – relative clauses – indirect statements …

Of course, it was most important that no one should see
Colin, Mary, or Dickon entering the secret garden. So Colin
gave orders to the gardeners that they must all keep away
from that part of the garden in future. *The Secret Garden*

STAGE 4 • 1400 HEADWORDS

… past perfect continuous – passive (simple forms) –
would conditional clauses – indirect questions –
relatives with *where/when* – gerunds after prepositions/phrases …

I was glad. Now Hyde could not show his face to the world
again. If he did, every honest man in London would be
proud to report him to the police. *Dr Jekyll and Mr Hyde*

STAGE 5 • 1800 HEADWORDS

… future continuous – future perfect –
passive (modals, continuous forms) –
would have conditional clauses – modals + perfect infinitive …

If he had spoken Estella's name, I would have hit him. I was so
angry with him, and so depressed about my future, that I could
not eat the breakfast. Instead I went straight to the old house.
Great Expectations

STAGE 6 • 2500 HEADWORDS

… passive (infinitives, gerunds) – advanced modal meanings –
clauses of concession, condition

When I stepped up to the piano, I was confident. It was as if I
knew that the prodigy side of me really did exist. And when I
started to play, I was so caught up in how lovely I looked that
I didn't worry how I would sound. *The Joy Luck Club*

BOOKWORMS · HUMAN INTEREST · STAGE 1
A Little Princess
FRANCES HODGSON BURNETT

Retold by Jennifer Bassett

Sara Crewe is a very rich little girl. She first comes to England when she is seven, and her father takes her to Miss Minchin's school in London. Then he goes back to his work in India. Sara is very sad at first, but she soon makes friends at school.

But on her eleventh birthday, something terrible happens, and now Sara has no family, no home, and not a penny in the world . .

BOOKWORMS · HUMAN INTEREST · STAGE 3
The Secret Garden
FRANCES HODGSON BURNETT

Retold by Clare West

Little Mary Lennox is a bad-tempered, disagreeable child. When her parents die in India, she is sent back to England to live with her uncle in a big, lonely, old house.

There is nothing to do all day except walk in the gardens – and watch the robin flying over the high walls of the secret garden . . . which has been locked for ten years. And no one has the key.